P9-CJC-029

THE VORTEX

A Play in Three Acts

By
NOEL COWARD

PUBLISHERS

HARPER & BROTHERS

NEW YORK AND LONDON

THE VORTEX

To

G. CALTHROP

WITH A GOOD DEAL OF GRATITUDE

DRAMATIS PERSONÆ

PRESTON

HELEN SAVILLE

PAUNCEFORT QUENTIN

CLARA HIBBERT

FLORENCE LANCASTER

TOM VERYAN

NICKY LANCASTER

DAVID LANCASTER

BUNTY MAINWARING

BRUSE FAIRLIGHT

THE VORTEX

ACT I

THE VORTEX

ACT I

The scene is the drawing-room of Mrs. Lancaster's *flat in London. The colors and decoration are on the verge of being original. The furniture is simple but distinctly expensive.*

Persons shown are Helen Saville *and* Pauncefort Quentin. Helen Saville *and* Pauncefort Quentin *are shown in by* Preston. Helen *is a smartly dressed woman of about thirty.* "Pawnie" *is an elderly maiden gentleman.*

Preston

I'm expecting Mrs. Lancaster in at any moment now, ma'am.

Helen

Thank you, Preston, we'll wait a little.

Preston

Shall I get you some tea?

3

HELEN

No, thanks, we've already had some—give me a cigarette, Pawnie; they're in that box on the table. [PAWNIE *hands her cigarette box*. PRESTON *goes out*.]

PAWNIE

It may be tiresome of me, but I think all this coloring is oppressive.

HELEN

You make such a " fetish " of house decoration, Pawnie.

PAWNIE

[*Wandering round the room*]
Not at all, but I do like things to be good and right.

HELEN

Well, I don't consider the new frieze in your bathroom either good or right.

PAWNIE

How can you, Helen! It's too marvelous for words. Parelli designed it specially for me.

HELEN

Personally, it would make me self-conscious to sit in a bath surrounded by frisky gods and goddesses all with such better figures than mine.

PAWNIE

I find it encouraging. This whole room is so typical of Florence.

HELEN

In what way?

PAWNIE

Every way.   Look at the furniture.

HELEN

A little artificial perhaps, but quite harmless.

PAWNIE

Dear Helen, you're such a loyal friend.

HELEN

I'm very fond of Florence.

PAWNIE

We all are.   Oh, my God, look at that lampshade!

HELEN

I gave it to her last Christmas.

PAWNIE

Wasn't that a little naughty of you?

HELEN

I don't see why; it's extremely pretty.

PAWNIE

Too unrestrained.   Such a bad example for the
servants.   [*He takes up frame from desk.*]   Who's
this boy?

HELEN

Tom Veryan.   You must have seen him.

PAWNIE

Florence's past, present, or future?

HELEN

Present.

PAWNIE

He has that innocent look that never fails to
attract elderly women.

HELEN

Don't be a cat.

PAWNIE

I wasn't meaning Florence; she's too divine to be
in any marked category.

HELEN

I wonder.

Pawnie

Oh, yes, Helen, deathless sort of magnetism, you know.

Helen

I often wonder what will happen to Florence eventually.

Pawnie

My dear, I'm far too occupied in wondering what's going to happen to me to worry about other people.

Helen

I've always thought your course was quite clear, Pawnie.

Pawnie

However offensive that remark was intended to be, Helen, I shall take it in the most complimentary spirit.

Helen

I'm sure you will.

Pawnie

I expect Florence will just go on and on, then suddenly become quite beautifully old, and go on and on still more.

HELEN

It's too late now for her to become beautifully old, I'm afraid. She'll have to be young indefinitely.

PAWNIE

I don't suppose she'll mind that, but it's trying for David.

HELEN

And fiendish for Nicky.

PAWNIE

Oh, no, my dear; you're quite wrong there. I'm sure Nicky doesn't care a damn.

HELEN

It's difficult to tell with Nicky.

PAWNIE

He's divinely selfish; all amusing people are.

HELEN

Did you hear him play in Paris?

PAWNIE

Yes.

HELEN

Well?

PAWNIE

Erratic—one or two things perfect, but he's slovenly.

HELEN

He only takes things seriously in spurts, but still he's very young.

PAWNIE

Do you really think that's a good excuse.

HELEN

No, I'm afraid not, especially when so much depends on it.

PAWNIE

What does depend on it?

HELEN

Everything—his life's happiness.

PAWNIE

Don't be so terribly intense, dear.

HELEN

It's true.

PAWNIE

I'm quite sure Nicky will be perfectly happy as long as he goes on attracting people; he loves being attractive.

HELEN

Naturally, he's Florence's son.

PAWNIE

Such an exciting thing to be.

HELEN

You don't believe Nicky's got anything in him at all, do you?

PAWNIE (*lightly*)

I don't think it matters, anyway.

HELEN

I do.

PAWNIE

But you've got a loving nature, Helen.   I always know it.

HELEN

Nicky hasn't had a chance.

PAWNIE

Nonsense—he's had everything he wanted ever since the day he was born, and he'll go on wasting his opportunities until he dies.

HELEN

Quite possibly.

PAWNIE

Well, there you are then.

HELEN

He may have had everything he wanted, but he's had none of the things he really needs.

PAWNIE

Are you talking socially or spiritually.

HELEN

You're quite right, Pawnie, you wouldn't be so beautifully preserved if you'd wasted any of your valuable time or sincerity.

PAWNIE

I forgive you for that, Helen, freely.

HELEN

Thank you so much.

PAWNIE

You must realize one thing, everyone is sacrificed to Florence—it's as it should be—of course, she's a couple of hundred years too late—she ought to have been a flaunting, intriguing King's mistress, with black page boys and jade baths and things too divine——

[*Enter* PRESTON.]

PRESTON

[*Announcing*]
Miss Hibbert.
[*Enter* CLARA HIBBERT—*she is affected, but quite
well dressed.* PRESTON *goes out.*]

CLARA

My *dears.* Isn't Florence back *yet?*

HELEN

No, we're waiting for her.

PAWNIE

You look harassed, Clara.

CLARA

I am harassed.

HELEN

Why?

CLARA

I'm singing to-night for Laura Tennant—she's
giving a dreadful reception at her dreadful house for
some dreadful Ambassador——

PAWNIE

How dreadful!

CLARA

No one will listen to me, of course—they'll all be far too busy avoiding the Cup and searching for the Champagne.

HELEN

What are you singing?

CLARA

One Gabriel Faure, two Reynaldo Hahn's and an Aria.

PAWNIE

Which Aria?

CLARA

I can't think, but my accompanist will know— I've got a frightful headache.

HELEN

Why don't you take off your hat?

CLARA

My dear, I daren't—I've just had my hair done —I suppose you haven't got a "Cachet Faivre," either of you?

HELEN

No, but Florence has, I expect—Preston will know where they are—ring the bell, Pawnie.

PAWNIE

[*Ringing bell*]
My poor Clara—I do hope your singing to-night will justify the fuss you're making this afternoon.

CLARA

Don't be so *brutal*, Pawnie.

HELEN

Is Gregory going with you?

CLARA

Of *course*—I *never* sing unless he's there—he gives me such marvelous moral support.

PAWNIE

"Moral" is hardly the word *I* should have chosen, dear.
[*Enter* PRESTON.]

HELEN

Do you know if Mrs. Lancaster has any "Cachet Faivre" anywhere?

PRESTON

Yes, ma'am—I think so.

CLARA

Do get me one, Preston, I'm suffering *tortures*.

PRESTON

Very well, miss.
[*She goes out.*]

PAWNIE

Preston has such wonderful poise, hasn't she?

HELEN

She needs it in this house.

CLARA

I do wish Florence would hurry up. I want to borrow her green fan. I've got a new Patou frock that positively *demands* it.

HELEN

She can't be long now.

CLARA

I suppose I daren't ask Preston for the fan and creep away with it?

HELEN

I shouldn't, if I were you—Florence is very touchy over that sort of thing.

CLARA

She promised it to me ages ago.

PAWNIE

Surely there isn't such a desperate hurry? You won't be singing until about half past eleven.

CLARA

[*Petulantly*]

My *dear*, I've got to *rehearse*—I don't know a word——

[*Re-enter* PRESTON *with a "Cachet Faivre" and a glass of water.*]

CLARA

You're a *saint*, Preston—thank you a *thousand* times——

PAWNIE

Soak it a little first, dear, or you'll choke, and I should *detest* that.

[CLARA *soaks "Cachet" and then swallows it.* PRESTON *goes out.*]

CLARA

Now I must lie down *flat*—get out of the way, Helen.

PAWNIE

Perhaps you'd like us *both* to go *right* out of the room and sit in the *hall?*

CLARA

No, Pawnie, I should never expect the least consideration from you.

[*She lies down flat on the divan,* HELEN *arranges cushions for her.*]

CLARA

Thank you, Helen darling—I shall always come to you whenever I'm ill.

HELEN

That *will* be nice.

[*Enter* FLORENCE LANCASTER *followed by* TOM VERYAN. FLORENCE *is brilliantly dressed almost to the point of being "outré." Her face still retains the remnants of great beauty.* TOM *is athletic and good-looking. One feels he is good at games and extremely bad at everything else.*]

FLORENCE

Helen—Pawnie, have you been here long?

PAWNIE

No, only a few hours.

FLORENCE

My dear. I'm so frightfully sorry—we've been held up for ages in the traffic. Davis is a congenital

idiot. Always manages to get to a turning just as
the policeman puts out his hand. No initiative whatever. What's happened to Clara? Has she been
run over?

CLARA

No, dear, I've got a frightful head.

FLORENCE

Pawnie, you know Tom, don't you?—Tom Veryan, Mr. Quentin, I'm sure you'll adore each other.

TOM

[*Shaking hands*]
How are you?

PAWNIE

Very well, thank you—how sweet of you to ask
me?

FLORENCE

Is there anything I can do, Clara?

CLARA

Yes, dear, lend me your green fan for to-night.

FLORENCE

All right—but you *won't* get too carried away
with it, will you, dear? I should hate the feathers
to come out. Does anyone want any tea?

HELEN

No thanks, dear.

FLORENCE

Cocktails, then?

PAWNIE

It's too early.

FLORENCE

[*Ringing bell*]
It's never too early for a cocktail.

CLARA

I should like to go quite quietly into a convent and never see anybody again ever——

PAWNIE

Gregory would be bored stiff in a convent.

FLORENCE

We've just been to a most frightful Charity *matinée*. Nothing but inaudible speeches from dreary old actors, and leading ladies nudging one another all over the stage. [PRESTON *enters*.] Cocktails, Preston, and ask Barker to wrap up my green fan for Miss Hibbert to take away with her.

PRESTON

Very good, ma'am.
[*She goes out.*]

CLARA

You're an angel, Florence—I think I'll sit up now.

FLORENCE

Do, dear, then Tom will be able to sit down.

CLARA

[*Sitting up*]
I really do feel most peculiar.

PAWNIE

You look far from normal, dear.

CLARA

If Pawnie's rude to me any more I shall burst into tears.

FLORENCE

Tom, give me a cigarette.

PAWNIE

Here are some.

FLORENCE

No, Tom has a special rather hearty kind that I adore.

CLARA

Lend me your lip stick, Helen; mine has sunk down into itself.

HELEN

Here you are.

CLARA

What a lovely color! I look far prettier than
I feel.

FLORENCE

[*To* TOM]
    Thank you, angel.

CLARA

I shan't be able to get down to the house until
Saturday evening, Florence—I'm seeing Gregory off
to Newcastle.

PAWNIE

Why Newcastle?

CLARA

His home's just near there—isn't it too awful for
him?

FLORENCE

Well, wire me the time of your train, won't you?

CLARA

Of course, dear.

HELEN

You're smelling divinely, Florence. What is it?

FLORENCE

[*Flicking her handkerchief*]
It is good, isn't it?

PAWNIE

"Narcisse Noir" of Caron.   I use it.

FLORENCE

Yes, you would, Pawnie.
[*Re-enter* PRESTON *with parcel.*]

PRESTON

Here is the fan, miss.

CLARA

[*Taking it*]
Thank you *so* much—you are sweet, Florence.   A
fan gives me such a feeling of *security* when I'm
singing modern stuff.   [PRESTON *goes out.*]   I must
rush now——

FLORENCE

Don't you want a cocktail before you go?

CLARA

No, darling—I should only hiccup all the evening.
Good-bye, you've been *such* a comfort—good-bye,
Helen—Pawnie, you will be nicer to me over the

week-end, won't you? I shall be *so* depressed, what
with Gregory going away and everything—Good-
bye, Tom—I shall dine in bed and give way at every
pore——
[*She goes out.*]

PAWNIE

Poor Clara—she eternally labors under the delu-
sion that she really matters.

HELEN

We all do that a little.

FLORENCE

[*Laughing*]
You're awfully cruel to her, Pawnie.

PAWNIE

She upsets my vibrations.

FLORENCE

[*Before glass*]
I've taken a sudden hatred to this hat. [*She
takes it off.*] That's better—are you going to the
"New Elaine" to-night, either of you?

HELEN

I'm not—but Pawnie is, of course.

PAWNIE

It's going to be *amazing*—what a cast, my dear!
Marvelous Selwyn Steele, Nora Dean, and that perfect woman, Lily Burfield——

HELEN

I can't stand her, she always over-acts.

PAWNIE

[*Incensed*]
How *can* you, Helen! Did you see her in "Simple
Faith"?

HELEN

Yes, unfortunately.

PAWNIE

Oh, you're really too tiresome for words!

HELEN

Her technique creaks like machinery.

PAWNIE

It's sacrilege—she's too, too marvelous.
[*Enter* PRESTON *with a tray of cocktails. All help
themselves.*]

FLORENCE

What do you think about it, Tom?

Tom

I've never seen her.

Florence

Yes, you have.   About three months ago, at the Comedy.

Tom

Oh. . . . I don't remember.

Pawnie

Don't remember!   An artist like that!   Good God, it's agony!

Helen

You'll look awfully tired at dinner-time, Pawnie, if you don't calm down a little.

Florence

This is special—my own invention.

Helen

Absolutely delicious.

Tom

A bit too sweet.

Florence

Tom, *darling*, don't be so **taciturn**—he's always taciturn after a *matinée*.

PAWNIE

When's Nicky coming back?

FLORENCE

To-morrow. Isn't it too divine? He's been away for a whole year, but I saw him for a moment on my way through Paris last month.

PAWNIE

Has he been working hard?

FLORENCE

I suppose so, but you know what Nicky is—bless his heart!

PAWNIE

I heard him play at Yvonne Mirabeau's.

FLORENCE

She's a loathsome woman, isn't she?

HELEN

Not as bad as that.

PAWNIE

She's a half-wit. I can't bear half-wits.

FLORENCE

She goes on so dreadfully about things—devastating.

PAWNIE

Funny Nicky liking her so much.

FLORENCE

Only because she keeps on saying how wonderful he is—that always appeals to Nicky.

PAWNIE

How old is he now?

FLORENCE

Twenty-four. Isn't it absurd to think I have such a grown-up son—old General Fenwick said last Thursday that—— [*The telephone rings; she goes to it.*] Hallo—hallo! Yes, my dear. How are you? . . . Yes, so am I, simply worn out. . . . No. When? How perfectly marvelous! . . . No, dear, it's a prescription; but I can let you have a little in a jar. . . . Quite easy. All you do is just rub it on at night. . . . Don't be so silly. . . . Not in the least; if you send the car round that will be all right. . . . Very well. . . . Good-bye, darling. [*She hangs up receiver.*] I give Clara Hibbert ten for stupidity. Don't you, Helen?

HELEN

A hundred and ten.

PAWNIE

Ten's the limit.

TOM

I say, Florence—I think I'd better be getting along if I've got to be dressed and back here by half past seven——

FLORENCE

You've got half an hour.

TOM

That's not very much.

FLORENCE

The car's outside . . . take it and send it straight back.

PAWNIE

Can it drop me, Florence dear? I always feel so much richer in your car than anyone else's.

FLORENCE

Of course, Pawnie.
[*The telephone rings again.*]

FLORENCE

[*At telephone*]
Hallo! . . . Yes . . . speaking. . . . How do you
do——?

PAWNIE

Good-bye, Helen.   It's been divine——

HELEN

Ring me up at tea-time to-morrow.

FLORENCE

How perfectly sweet of you! . . . Now, now,
really. . . . Well, naturally, if you persist in saying
such charming things . . . [*laughing gayly*] . . .
What nonsense! . . .

PAWNIE

Good-bye, Florence——

FLORENCE

[*She puts her hand over mouthpiece*]
It's that awful General Fenwick. . . . Good-bye,
Pawnie dear.   You're coming down to the house on
Friday?

PAWNIE

Yes; too lovely——

FLORENCE

Helen's coming by the five-o'clock—you'd better travel together.

PAWNIE

Perfect. [*To* TOM.] Are you ready?

TOM

Quite.

PAWNIE

[*As they go out*]
You *can* drop me first, can't you? I'm not as young as I was——

FLORENCE

[*At telephone*]
Please forgive me. People rushing in and out, this house grows more like a railway station every day. . . . Now, General, that was a deliberate compliment. [*She laughs.*] Ridiculous man. . . . Very well. . . . Good-bye. [*She hangs up receiver.*] My God! ten for dreariness!

HELEN

He's not a bad old thing.

FLORENCE

No, but he tries to be, and that's what's so frightful. [*Arranging her hair before glass.*] I look like Death. . . . Isn't Tom a darling?

HELEN

Yes, dear, without being aggressively brilliant.

FLORENCE

I'm afraid, Helen, you're getting rather bitter.

HELEN

Nonsense.

FLORENCE

It's silly to be sarcastic about Tom.

HELEN

It's better than being maudlin about him.

FLORENCE

I don't know what you mean, dear. I'm not in the least maudlin, and never have been about anybody. I sometimes wish I could be—I'm too hard.

HELEN

[*Taking a cigarette*]
Tom will let you down.

FLORENCE

Let me down? Why . . . how . . . I don't
understand——

HELEN

You're more in love with him than he is with you.

FLORENCE

Don't be so *absurd*, Helen.

HELEN

It's true.

FLORENCE

[*Complacently*]
He adores me—worships me—he's never seen anyone like me before in his life. I'm something strange
. . . exotic——

HELEN

You're more in love with him than he is with you.

FLORENCE

You're getting on my nerves to-day, Helen.

HELEN

You do see that I'm right, don't you?

FLORENCE

If you knew some of the things he's said to me.

HELEN

I can guess them.

FLORENCE

That boy was utterly unawakened until he met me.

HELEN

He's very young.

FLORENCE

I've taught him—everything.

HELEN

Or nothing.

FLORENCE

Helen, I believe you're jealous.

HELEN

Don't be a fool.

FLORENCE

I wish I hadn't this fatal knack of seeing through people.

HELEN

How's David?

FLORENCE

I don't know. He ought to be home soon.

HELEN

Doesn't he ever suspect anything?

FLORENCE

Of course not—he adores me.

HELEN

It seems so strange not to see——

FLORENCE

I'm devoted to David—I'd do anything for him, anything in the world—but he's grown old and I've kept young; it does muddle things up so. I can't help having a temperament, can I?

HELEN

Temperament. . . . No.

FLORENCE

David's always loved me and never understood me —you see, I'm such an extraordinary *mixture*. I have so many *sides* to my character. I adore being at home and running the house and looking after David and Nicky——

HELEN

You don't exactly overdo it.

FLORENCE

Well, Nicky's been away for such ages. Also, one must be in London for the season. You can't expect me to bury myself in the country indefinitely. I shall be there practically all through the spring and summer.

HELEN

Lovely tennis parties and cricket weeks and things——

FLORENCE

Certainly.

HELEN

[*Kissing her*]
You're a divine creature, Florence.

FLORENCE

[*Basking*]
Am I? [*The telephone rings.*] Hallo! . . . Yes—speaking. [*To* HELEN *in a whisper.*] It's Inez Zulieta. I never went to her recital. . . . Inez *darling*, I never recognized your voice. . . . Didn't you get my note? . . . It was absolutely true, I was in agony. . . . Inez, don't be angry. If you only knew how I longed for the sound of your wonderful, wonderful voice. . . . Darling. . . . Inez, don't be

so cruel. . . . To-morrow, then. [*She hangs up receiver.*] I do wish Inez wasn't so persistent.

HELEN

You never stop encouraging her.

FLORENCE

Oh, Helen, I'm so tired of everyone.

HELEN

Except Tom?

FLORENCE

Yes, except Tom; he's such a darling.

HELEN

How do you think he and Nicky will get on?

FLORENCE

Marvelously—Tom loves music.

HELEN

He says he does.

FLORENCE

My dear, I took him to that Russian thing the other day and he sat entranced from beginning to end.

HELEN

Poor Nicky!

FLORENCE

Why do you say that?

HELEN

Because I sometimes feel it.

FLORENCE

[*Suddenly furious*]
Oh, I wonder why we're such friends—we're so opposite—you don't understand me a bit. I used to think you did, but you've been different lately—unsympathetic.

HELEN

No, I haven't.

FLORENCE

Yes, you have—over Tom—I believe you're in love with him yourself.

HELEN

[*Smiling*]
No—it isn't that.

FLORENCE

Anyhow, you can't bear him being in love with me.

Helen

I don't think he is—really. I quite realize that he *was* very violently infatuated, but that is wearing off a bit now. I'm beginning to see him as he is. . . .

Florence

No, no, it's not true—you don't understand——

Helen

We *are* friends, Florence, though we're so "opposite." Do you really know the truth—inside you? Or is all this shrill vanity real?

Florence

What's the matter with you?

Helen

You're ten years older than I am, but when I'm your age I shall be twenty years older than you.

Florence

Darling, how deliciously involved—what *can* you mean by that?

Helen

I mean, I think it's silly not to grow old when the time comes.

[*She rises and goes towards door.*]

FLORENCE

[*Outraged*]

Helen! [*There is suddenly heard a violent knocking at the front door.*] What on earth is that?

[*There is a noise outside, then the door bursts open and* NICKY *enters. He is extremely well dressed in traveling clothes. He is tall and pale, with thin, nervous hands.*]

FLORENCE

Nicky!

NICKY

Mother!

[*He embraces her.*]

FLORENCE

But I'd no idea—I thought you were coming to-morrow.

NICKY

No, to-day—I wrote to you.

FLORENCE

I'm terribly, terribly excited.

NICKY

Helen, dear, how are you?

[*He kisses her.*]

HELEN

Splendid, Nicky.

FLORENCE

I can't get over you arriving like this. . . . I never realized——

NICKY

Silly . . . you're looking awfully well.

FLORENCE

Am I?

NICKY

Wonderful, as usual.

FLORENCE

I was talking to George Morrison only last Thursday——

NICKY

The man who wrote that fearful book?

FLORENCE

It isn't a fearful book, it's brilliant—anyhow, he absolutely refused to believe that I had a grown-up son.

HELEN

My dears, I must fly.

NICKY

Don't go yet.

HELEN

I must—I'm hours late as it is.

NICKY

Be a little later, then.

FLORENCE

Remember, five o'clock train on Friday.

NICKY

Oh, is she coming down to the house? Divine!

HELEN

Yes, if Florence is still speaking to me. Good-bye.
[*She goes out.*]

NICKY

Have you been having a scene?

FLORENCE

No, dear.

NICKY

She's a darling—Helen——

FLORENCE

Extremely stupid and tactless sometimes.

NICKY

It doesn't feel as though I'd been away at all.

FLORENCE

I've missed you appallingly—we had such a short time together in Paris. Did you enjoy all my letters?

NICKY

I adored them—so did John Bagot. I used to read most of them aloud to him. He's mad on you—saw your pictures in the *Tatler*, or something, and fell in love with it.

FLORENCE

Is he nice?

NICKY

He's grand.

FLORENCE

We must all dine at the Embassy. When is he coming to England?

NICKY

Not until after Christmas.

FLORENCE

You must see my new photographs; they're wonderful.

[*She takes large packet from desk.*]

NICKY

It's heavenly—being back.

FLORENCE

Look.

NICKY

I don't like that one.

FLORENCE

How can you, Nicky! Tom likes that one best of all.

NICKY

Who's Tom?

FLORENCE

Tom Veryan—he's a dear; you'll like him frightfully—you know—the very nicest type of Englishman.

NICKY

I hate the very nicest type of Englishman.

FLORENCE

Don't be tiresome, Nicky; he's only twenty-four, and they all think *so* well of him——

NICKY

All who?

FLORENCE

All his officers and people; he's in the Brigade.

NICKY

[*Holding photograph away from him and scrutinizing it through half-closed eyes*]

Now that one really is *enchanting*——they've got your hair *beautifully*.. Oh, yes, my dear, it's perfect——

FLORENCE

[*Complacently*]

It *is* good. She's sweet——Madame Henderson, she simply won't hear of my paying for these——she says it's quite sufficient to be allowed to exhibit them in the window.

NICKY

Is anyone dining this evening?

FLORENCE

No. Oh, dear! I'd forgotten——I'm dining out with Tom.

NICKY

Oh—I see.

FLORENCE

Your first night home, too—how perfectly fiendish. What a fool I am to have muddled it up.

NICKY

It doesn't matter, darling.

FLORENCE

Oh, but it *does*. I wonder if we could get another seat——

NICKY

Seat? What for?

FLORENCE

We're going to the first night of "The New Elaine." It's going to be marvelous.

NICKY

Who's in it?

FLORENCE

Nora Dean and Selwyn Steele——

NICKY

Oh, God!

FLORENCE

It's silly of you *always* to jeer at Selwyn Steele. He's a brilliant actor, if only he could get away from his wife. . . .

NICKY

I couldn't bear him to-night, anyway; I'm tired. Is father home yet?

FLORENCE

No, I don't think so. Oh, I do feel such a beast——

NICKY

Don't be silly—honestly, I don't mind a bit.

FLORENCE

I know—you have a nice quiet dinner here and join us at the Embassy afterwards.

NICKY

Is it a late night?

FLORENCE

Yes, they play the most heavenly tune there now— Tom always makes them do it over and over again— I'll put it on——
[*She goes to the gramophone.*]

NICKY

How's Iris?

FLORENCE

My dear, don't speak of her.

NICKY

Why—what's she done?

FLORENCE

She's been absolutely foul.

NICKY

In what way?

FLORENCE

Every way—I never trusted her, luckily—Thank God I've got instincts about people—listen, isn't this marvelous—She said the most filthy things to Gloria Craig about me—I always knew she was insanely jealous, but there are limits. I loathe being at people's beck and call. . . . Come and dance.

NICKY

[*As they dance*]
I'm sorry you've rowed—I rather liked her——

FLORENCE

Only because she kept on saying how wonderful you were. . . . She doesn't know a thing about music really.

NICKY

Oh yes, she does.

FLORENCE

It's merely bluff—all that appreciation. *Darling,* how oddly you're dancing.

NICKY

It's probably because we haven't danced together for so long. . . .

FLORENCE

Anyhow, now she's gone off to Monte Carlo with Violet Fenchurch—silly fool——
[*Enter* DAVID LANCASTER. *He is an elderly gray-haired pleasant man.*]

DAVID

[*Delighted*]
Nicky—my boy——

NICKY

[*Kissing him*]
Hallo, father——

DAVID

I thought—Florence said—to-morrow——

NICKY

Mother muddled it up.

DAVID

You look rather tired.

NICKY

I'm splendid.   How's everything?

DAVID

The same as usual.   I've made lots of improvements down at the house.

FLORENCE

David thinks and talks of nothing but the farm——

DAVID

It's beginning to pay a bit—Peterson's an awfully good man.

NICKY

We'll make a grand tour of it on Sunday.

DAVID

Have you enjoyed yourself in Paris?

NICKY

Oh yes, rather—it's a splendid place to work.

DAVID

It never struck me that way quite, but still——

FLORENCE

Sophie de Molignac said Nicky's playing had improved wonderfully.

DAVID

I'm so glad, Nicky.

NICKY

I've been doing some Spanish stuff lately.

DAVID

I wish I knew more about it.

NICKY

Never mind, father.

DAVID

Come to my room and talk. I can't bear that thing——

FLORENCE

Father's such a beast; he never will dance with me.

DAVID

Is the *Evening News* anywhere about?

NICKY

Yes, here.
[*He gives it to him.*]

DAVID

I'm so glad you're home again, Nicky—don't forget—come and talk. . . .
[*He goes out.*]

FLORENCE

David's so much happier in the country.

NICKY

Why on earth doesn't he retire and live at the house for good?

FLORENCE

Work has become such a habit with him—he's always hated giving up habits.

NICKY

Mother—I've got something rather important to tell you.

FLORENCE

Darling, how thrilling! What is it?

NICKY

I am engaged to be married.

FLORENCE

What!

NICKY

Practically—as much as one can be these days.

FLORENCE

Nicky!

NICKY

Don't look so stricken.

FLORENCE

But, Nicky—I never sort of visualized you being engaged, or married, or anything.

NICKY

Why not?

FLORENCE

You're not old enough.

NICKY

I'm twenty-four.

FLORENCE

You don't look it. . . . Thank God!

NICKY

What do you really feel about it, mother?

FLORENCE

Darling—I hardly know what to say—you've sprung it on me so suddenly. Who is she?

NICKY

A girl called Bunty Mainwaring.

FLORENCE

What a silly name!

NICKY

It isn't at all—it's very attractive.

FLORENCE

Is she an actress, or a student, or what?

NICKY

Neither—she is what is technically termed a "lady."

FLORENCE

Do you think she'll like me?

NICKY

She went mad over your photograph.

FLORENCE

Which one?

NICKY

The "looking out of the window" one.

FLORENCE

That really is one of the best I've ever had done.

NICKY

She said you had the face of an heroic little boy.

FLORENCE

What a *divine* thing to say!
[*She glances at herself in the glass.*]

NICKY

She does say divine things—she's supremely intelligent.

FLORENCE

Is she in Paris?

NICKY

No, she came over with me to-day.

FLORENCE

Where does she live?

NICKY

Just round the corner in Carbury Square.

FLORENCE

Near the Churchingtons.

NICKY

It's her mother's house, but her mother's away just now, so I asked her to change quickly and come on here.

FLORENCE

Nicky!

NICKY

Why not? I wanted you to see her as soon as possible.

FLORENCE

[*Realizing parental responsibility*]
It's an awful shock, you know.

NICKY

Nonsense, mother—you're quite excited about it, really.

FLORENCE

[*With determination*]
I shall be charming to her.

NICKY

Then she'll adore you at once—probably too much, and I shall be jealous.

FLORENCE

You'd better both dine here together and come on to the Embassy. How old is she?

NICKY

Twenty-three.

FLORENCE

What does she do?

NICKY

Nothing much—she writes things occasionally.

FLORENCE

Where did you meet her?

NICKY

First of all at a party at Olive Lloyd-Kennedy's.

FLORENCE

I can't bear Olive Lloyd-Kennedy—she's a cat.

NICKY

Then I met her again at Marion Fawcett's—a frightful sort of reception affair—she was staying with her.

FLORENCE

She seems to move exclusively with my worst ene-mies.   Is she pretty?

NICKY

I don't know—I haven't really noticed.

FLORENCE

[*With a touch of real feeling*]
Nicky darling, I do feel so extraordinary about it.

NICKY

Why extraordinary?

FLORENCE

It's a milestone, isn't it—you being engaged?   A definite milestone?   [*She catches sight of herself.*] Look at my nose.   [*She powders it.*]   I do hope she'll like me—I must go and dress now; Tom is fetching me half-past seven.   Bring her to my room when she comes.

NICKY

Don't go for a minute.

FLORENCE

I must, really—Tom will be furious.

NICKY

Oh, damn Tom!

FLORENCE

Oh, Nicky, *don't* go and take one of your tiresome prejudices against him.

NICKY

[*Smiling*]
All right, I'll try not to.

FLORENCE

He's frightfully good-looking.

NICKY

Oh!

FLORENCE

And he adores music.

NICKY

Now, then, mother——

FLORENCE

He does, honestly.

NICKY

Good.

FLORENCE

And he dances beautifully.

NICKY

I shall never stop dancing with him.

FLORENCE

And he's so good at games.

NICKY

He sounds adorable.

FLORENCE

Of course, he needs knowing.

NICKY

So do I.

FLORENCE

You will make an effort, though, darling, won't you? For my sake!

NICKY

Yes, mother.

FLORENCE

And we'll all have a divine time together, Tom and me and you and what's her name——

NICKY

Bunty.

FLORENCE

Oh yes, of course, Bunty.
[*Front door bell rings.*]

NICKY

This is her, I expect.

FLORENCE

Do you feel wonderful about her?

NICKY

Yes.

FLORENCE

It is thrilling, isn't it—being in love?

NICKY

[*Frowning a little*]
Yes.

FLORENCE

Your father was right—you look awfully tired,
Nicky.

NICKY

What nonsense! I feel grand.
[*Enter* PRESTON.]

PRESTON

[*Announcing*]
Miss Mainwaring.
[BUNTY *comes in, very self-assured and well-dressed.
    She is more attractive than pretty in a boyish
    sort of way.*]
[PRESTON *goes out.*]

NICKY

Bunty.   You have been quick.

BUNTY

I've simply flown.

NICKY

Bunty . . . here is mother. . . .

BUNTY

Oh!

FLORENCE

[*Taking both her hands*]
This is frightfully exciting, isn't it?
[*She kisses her.*]

NICKY

I've told her.

BUNTY

Are you furious?

FLORENCE

Of course not.   Why should I be?   'Specially now.

BUNTY

It's absolutely incredible, you being Nicky's mother.

FLORENCE

Am I anything like you thought I'd be?

BUNTY

Yes, exactly—but I couldn't believe it until I saw you.

FLORENCE

Take off that perfectly divine cloak and have a cigarette.   I've got to rush and dress now, because I'm *terribly* late, but you're dining here with Nicky and joining Tom Veryan and me at the Embassy afterwards.

BUNTY

Tom Veryan? . . .

FLORENCE

Yes.   Do you know him?

BUNTY

I did when I was a child—if it's the same one.
[*She takes off her cloak.*]

FLORENCE

[*Effusively*]
Nicky—I don't feel extraordinary about it any
more—I'm *delighted*.

NICKY

Angel.

FLORENCE

Perhaps Bunty would like to come down to the
house on Friday for the week-end?

NICKY

Oh yes! Marvelous.

BUNTY

It's awfully sweet of you, Mrs. Lancaster.

FLORENCE

You must call me Florence; I can't bear Mrs.
Lancaster. I must fly; Tom will be here at any
moment—that's him on the desk.

BUNTY

[*Going over to photograph*]
Yes—it is the same one.

FLORENCE

How too divine! . . .
[*Telephone rings.*]
Hallo! . . . Yes, speaking! . . . Elsa darling, how
are you? . . . What? . . . To-night? . . . How per-
fectly heavenly! Of course, I'd adore it. . . . Lis-
ten. Nicky's just back from Paris. Can he come,
too, with Bunty Mainwaring? . . . Yes, he's here.
. . . See you to-night, dear. . . .
Here, Nicky, talk to Elsa. . . .
[*She snatches up her hand-bag and fur coat and
kisses* BUNTY *effusively.*]
I'm so glad about you and Nicky—It's too wonder-
ful.
[*She rushes out.*]

NICKY

[*At telephone*]
Hallo, Elsa. . . . I'd no idea you were in London.
I'm terribly thrilled. My dear, you haven't. . . .
All those lovely tunes you played to me in Paris?
. . . *How amazing!* I *am* glad. . . . Have you
done anything with that Tango? . . . You must
play it tonight; I want Bunty to hear it. . . . It is

perfect, isn't it? . . . Good-bye, dear. [*He hangs up the receiver*.] Bunty.

BUNTY

What?

NICKY

I'm terribly happy.

BUNTY

So am I.

NICKY

Do you remember how we planned all this—coming home together—and breaking it to mother—and everything?

BUNTY

Rather.

NICKY

Do you really like her?

BUNTY

I adore her—she's a perfect angel.

NICKY

I told her your "heroic little boy" line; she loved it.

BUNTY

It's true, you know—rather defiant too—laughing at Fate.

NICKY

Doesn't Paris seem ages away now?

BUNTY

A different life altogether.

NICKY

That nasty little bit of Channel is such an enormous gulf, really.   Did you put that dress on on purpose.

BUNTY

[*Smiling*]
Perhaps.

NICKY

You are a devil.

BUNTY

It's such fun being reminded of things.

NICKY

And such agony, too.

BUNTY

Nicky darling—why agony?

NICKY

It's always agony being in love, and I started loving you in that dress.

BUNTY

Did you?

NICKY

Don't pretend you didn't know.

BUNTY

I suppose one always knows—really.

NICKY

From the very first moment.

BUNTY

Yes.

NICKY

A sort of spark.

BUNTY

Your playing helped a lot.

NICKY

I meant it to.

BUNTY

Calculating pig.

NICKY

Have a cigarette?

BUNTY

All right.
[*He hands her box, and she takes one.*]

NICKY

[*Lighting her cigarette*]
I wish we weren't so free.

BUNTY

Why?   What do you mean?

NICKY

I feel I should like to elope, or something violently romantic like that.

BUNTY

[*Laughing*]
There wouldn't be much point in it now, would there?

NICKY

Perhaps not.   How much do you love me?

BUNTY

I don't know.

NICKY

It's fun analyzing one's emotions.

BUNTY

Marvelous fun.

NICKY

And a comfort, too, when things go wrong—but it kills sentiment stone dead.

BUNTY

A good job, too.

NICKY

You're frightfully hard, Bunty.

BUNTY

Am I?

NICKY

Much harder than me—really.

BUNTY

You've got so much hysteria.

NICKY

I can't help it.

BUNTY

Of course not; it's your temperament.   You burst out suddenly.

NICKY

Not so badly as I used to.

BUNTY

You're growing older.

NICKY

God, yes!   Isn't it foul?

BUNTY

Hell, my dear.

NICKY

It's funny how mother's generation always longed to be old when they were young, and we strain every nerve to keep young.

BUNTY

That's because we see what's coming so much more clearly.

NICKY

Wouldn't it be terrible to know *exactly?*—I feel frightened sometimes.

BUNTY

Why?

NICKY

We're all so hectic and nervy. . . .

BUNTY

It doesn't matter—it probably only means we shan't live so long. . . .

NICKY

[*Suddenly*]
Shut up—shut up. . . .
[*Enter* Preston.]

PRESTON

[*Announcing*]
Mr. Veryan.
[*Enter* Tom. Nicky *greets him and shakes hands.*
Exit Preston.]

NICKY

How are you? I'm Nicky—I came over to-day instead of to-morrow. . . .

TOM

Oh!

NICKY

Do you know Bunty Mainwaring?

TOM

Bunty—I say—I am glad.
[*They shake hands warmly.*]

NICKY

We'd better have some cocktails.
[*He goes to the door and shouts.*]
Preston . . . bring us some cocktails. . . .

TOM

This *is* jolly. I didn't know what had become
of you.

BUNTY

I've been living in Paris a good deal.

TOM

How many years ago is it since we . . .

BUNTY

During the War. The last time I saw you you
were at Sandhurst.

NICKY

Such a pretty place.

TOM

You've hardly altered a bit—more grown up, of
course.

NICKY

All this is most affecting.

TOM

Bunty and I used to know each other awfully
well.

NICKY

What fun!

BUNTY

[*Warningly*]
Nicky . . .

NICKY

But it is—it's thrilling—there's nothing so charm-
ng as a reunion.

BUNTY

Nicky and I have been traveling all day. . . .
Boats and trains get on his nerves. . . .

NICKY

When the cocktails come, tell Preston to bring
mine to me in father's room.

BUNTY

Nicky, don't be so silly.

NICKY

Surely it's not silly to want to talk to my aged
father after a year's debauch in Paris? I fail to
see why you should have the monopoly of reunions.

BUNTY

Well, don't be long.

TOM

Cheerio!

NICKY

[*Crossly*]
Oh, God!
[*He goes out.*]

TOM

What's up?

BUNTY

These temperamental musicians.

TOM

Silly ass.

BUNTY

He isn't really—he's only jealous.

TOM

Why . . . is he . . .?

BUNTY

We're by way of being engaged.

TOM

What?

BUNTY

Why not?

TOM

Are you . . . are you in love with him?

BUNTY

[*Lightly*]
Yes—isn't it damnable?

TOM

Good Lord!
[*He laughs.*]

BUNTY

What are you laughing at?

TOM

It seems so funny you being in love with that sort
of chap.

BUNTY

What do you mean by "that sort of chap"?

TOM

Oh—I don't know, that type seems so unlike you.

BUNTY

Type?

TOM

Yes, you know—up in the air—effeminate.

BUNTY

You're more bucolic than you used to be, Tom.

TOM

Here, I say. . . .
[*Enter* Preston *with cocktails.*]

BUNTY

Will you please take Mr. Nicky's in to him in his father's room?

PRESTON

Yes, miss.

TOM

Is Mrs. Lancaster nearly ready?

PRESTON

I think so, sir.

TOM

Ask her to hurry.   We shall be late.

PRESTON

Yes, sir.
[*He goes out.*]

BUNTY

I can laugh now.
[*She does so.*]

TOM

Why?

BUNTY

I've just realized something.

TOM

What?

BUNTY

We shall meet again—over the week-end.

TOM

Are you coming down to the house?

BUNTY

Yes.

TOM

That's splendid. Come for a tramp Sunday
morning and we'll talk.

BUNTY

What about?

TOM

Oh, lots of things—old times.

BUNTY

[*Lifting her cocktail*]
Old times, Tom.

TOM

[*Doing the same*]
Cheerio!

CURTAIN

ACT II

ACT II

The scene is the hall of Mrs. Lancaster's *house, about forty miles from London.*

When the curtain rises it is just after dinner on the Sunday of the week-end party—the gramophone is going and there is a continual buzz of conversation. Clara Hibbert, *an emaciated soprano, is dancing with* Tom Veryan, Helen *with* Pawnie, *and* Nicky *with* Bunty. Florence *is seated on the club fender, talking intellectually with* Bruce Fairlight, *an earnest dramatist, the squalor of whose plays is much appreciated by those who live in comparative luxury.*

There must be a feeling of hectic amusement and noise, and the air black with cigarette smoke and superlatives. During the first part of the scene everyone must appear to be talking at once, but the actual lines spoken while dancing must be timed to reach the audience as the speakers pass near the footlights. This scene will probably be exceedingly difficult to produce, but is absolutely indispensable.

HELEN

It's much too fast, Nicky.

TOM

Do slow down a bit.

NICKY

It's the pace that's marked on the record.

PAWNIE

I've never danced well since the War, I don't know why.

FLORENCE

But your last act was so strong, when she came in half mad with fright and described everything minutely.

BRUCE

I try to write as *honestly* as possible.

CLARA

I gave her three for manners, but seven for charm, because I had to be a *little* nice!

TOM

I thought she was rather a decent sort.

BUNTY

No, but really, Nicky, his technique completely annihilated his inspiration.

NICKY

Not with Debussy and Ravel, with the older masters, yes; but he's probably tired of them.

BUNTY

That's so stupid, I think.

HELEN

My dear, it was the most "chic" thing you've ever seen, but unfortunately the wrong color.

PAWNIE

Marion Ferris had that Poiret model copied in the most frightful blue!

CLARA

I believe my shoe's coming off.

TOM

Shall we stop?

CLARA

No, it's all right.

FLORENCE

I wonder if you could gouge this cigarette-end out of the holder for me?

BRUCE

I'll try. [*He does so.*]   I always smoke a pipe when I'm working.

FLORENCE

How soothing!

BUNTY

I suppose one can never really judge properly from a recital.

NICKY

Not with him, because he's not dramatic enough.

BUNTY

Dramatic pianists make me uncomfortable.

HELEN

Pawnie, your tongue grows more venomous every day.

PAWNIE

[*Giggling*]
Well, I had to say something—anyhow, it was true.

HELEN

Especially about her ankles.

PAWNIE

My dear, yes!
[*They both laugh.*]
[*The record comes to an end, and* NICKY *begins to change it. Everyone talks and laughs.*]

CLARA

You must come next Sunday week.

TOM

Thanks awfully, I'd love to.

CLARA

I'm only singing ballads, but you know what Sunday concerts are.

TOM

Oh yes, rather.

CLARA

[*To* NICKY]
What's on the other side?

NICKY

"You've got the cutest ears and eyes and nose."

PAWNIE

Do put on "Spoony Moon in Upper Carolina."

HELEN

No, don't put it on, Nicky; play it yourself; you always make the gramophone go too quickly.

BUNTY

Yes, go on, Nicky.

FLORENCE

[*Refusing* BRUCE's *offer of a cigarette*]
No, thanks, not another—I'm dancing with Tom.

BUNTY

[*Gayly*]
Missing one, Tom.

TOM

Righto!
[NICKY *commences to play a fox-trot.*]

BUNTY

[*Dragging* BRUCE *to his feet*]
Come on, Mr. Fairlight, don't overdo the serious dramatist stunt!

BRUCE

I warn you I'm no good.
[*He dances with her, and confirms the truth of his warning.* CLARA HIBBERT *squashes down on*

the piano-seat next to NICKY *and endeavors with
one finger in the treble to follow the tune he is
playing.* HELEN *and* PAWNIE *stand right down
close to the footlights, smoking and talking;
their backs are half turned to the audience, but
their remarks must be perfectly audible.*]

HELEN

Tom Veryan doesn't dance as well as he thinks
he does.

PAWNIE

With that figure he ought to be marvelous.

HELEN

He's too athletic.

PAWNIE

Anyhow, I'm sure he's a success at the Bath Club.

HELEN

Doesn't Florence look astounding?

PAWNIE

Absolutely.   She knows exactly what suits her.

HELEN

Where's David?

PAWNIE

He went off to his study to smoke.

HELEN

I do wish Florence wouldn't be irritable with him in front of everybody.   I felt acutely uncomfortable at dinner.

PAWNIE

It makes Nicky furious as a rule, but to-night he was too occupied with that stupid little fool Bunty Mainwaring to take any notice.

HELEN

She's an excellent type.

PAWNIE

Very average; I only hope nothing will come of Nicky's mania for her.

HELEN

I don't think we need worry.

PAWNIE

Why?

HELEN

Wait and see, my dear.

CLARA

[*Leaving* NICKY *at the piano and advancing on* PAWNIE]
Come and dance, Pawnie, and tell me how divinely I sang on Tuesday.

PAWNIE

[*Agreeably*]
You didn't.

CLARA

Ten for cruelty.
[*They start to dance.* HELEN *moves over to the mantelpiece for a cigarette.*]

HELEN

Have you a match, Nicky?

NICKY

Isn't this a marvelous tune?

HELEN

Fascinating! [*She goes over and sits next to him. Gently slipping her hand into his coat pocket.*] Darling, I *do* want a match. [*She brings out a little box.*] What a divine little box!
[NICKY *stops playing and jumps up.*]

NICKY

[*Violently*]
Helen, give that to me!——
[*Everyone stops dancing.*]

CLARA

Nicky dear, *don't* be tiresome.

NICKY

[*Recovering himself.*]
I'm sick of playing. Let's have the gramophone
again. [*To* HELEN.] Here's a light, dearie.
[*He takes match-box out of another pocket and
lights* HELEN's *cigarette. She looks at him
queerly for a moment, then he restarts the
gramophone and everyone begins to dance again
except* HELEN *and* BRUCE FAIRLIGHT. HELEN
*goes over to the fireplace and takes a coffee-cup
from the mantelpiece.*]

HELEN

Whose coffee is this? Some one drank mine,
and I'd hardly touched it.

BRUCE

If it had no sugar in it, it's mine.

Helen

[*Draining it*]
It had no sugar in it.

Florence

You're dancing abominably, Tom.

Tom

Oh, Am I?

Florence

What's the matter with you?

Tom

I don't know.   I suppose I'm tired.

Florence

You're not usually tired when you're dancing
with me.

Tom

Oh, Florence, don't nag!

Florence

How dare you speak to me like that?
[*She stops dancing and goes over to the fireplace.*]

Tom

[*Following her*]
I say, Florence—I'm sorry——

PAWNIE

Let's stop the music for a moment and think of something really marvelous to do.

BUNTY

No, let's go on dancing.

CLARA

I'm exhausted.

PAWNIE

[*Stopping the gramophone*]
What was that divine game we played coming back from Paris, Helen?

HELEN

Just ordinary "Clumps," wasn't it?

BUNTY

I loathe "Clumps."

NICKY

What about the History game?

BRUCE

What's that?

BUNTY

Oh no, Nicky; it's too intellectual.

FLORENCE

There's a Mah-Jong set in the drawing-room.

PAWNIE

How divine! Let's make up a table immediately.

CLARA

I won't be happy until some one gives me a set made entirely of jade.

NICKY

Come on, Bunty.

BUNTY

[*Looking at* TOM]
I can't play it.

NICKY

You can; you used to play in Paris with Yvonne.

BUNTY

I've forgotten it.

NICKY

You'll soon remember again.
[*He drags her off.*]

PAWNIE

Come along, Clara.

CLARA

I insist on Mr. Fairlight learning.

BRUCE

I'm afraid I'm no good at that sort of thing.

CLARA

You'll be able to put it in one of your plays.

PAWNIE

Come and watch; it's too thrilling for words.
[CLARA, BRUCE *and* PAWNIE *go off*.]

HELEN

Have you only one set, Florence?

FLORENCE

Yes. Isn't it maddening? Clara promised to
bring hers down, but forgot.

HELEN

Does Bruce Fairlight play Bridge?

FLORENCE

No, I don't think so.

HELEN

Dramatists are such a comfort in a house party,
aren't they?
[*She goes off*.]

TOM

Are you coming, Florence?

FLORENCE

No.

TOM

[*Nonplussed*]
Oh!

FLORENCE

But please don't let me stop *you* going. I'm sure you're *dying* to be with the others.

TOM

I say, Florence, I wish you wouldn't go on like that.

FLORENCE

I don't know what's the matter with you; you've never behaved like this before.

TOM

I haven't behaved like anything.

FLORENCE

You've been exceedingly rude to me, both at dinner and afterwards.

Tom

I wasn't at dinner.

Florence

Yes, you were; you snapped me up when I said I didn't like Elsie Saunders.

Tom

You know perfectly well she's a friend of mine.

Florence

Well, she oughtn't to be, after the things she's said about me.

Tom

You will go on imagining.

Florence

Nothing of the sort—I *know!* If you weren't so dense you'd see, too—the jealousy I have to put up with. I get so tired of it all, so desperately tired. [*She becomes a little pathetic.*]

Tom

Talk about being different, you're different too——

Florence

I'm unhappy.

TOM

Why?

FLORENCE

Because I hate to see you being put against me.

TOM

Florence!

FLORENCE

You'll understand one day. They're all very subtle, but I can see.

TOM

Nobody's said a word to me about you; they'd better not try.

FLORENCE

Why, what would you do?

TOM

I'd—I'd be furious.

FLORENCE

Oh!

TOM

And I'd let them see it, too.

FLORENCE

[*Holding out her hands*]
Tom——

TOM

Yes?

FLORENCE

I forgive you.

TOM

I can't bear you being angry with me.

FLORENCE

Can't you, really?

TOM

It makes me feel beastly.

FLORENCE

Come and sit here.

TOM

[*Sitting next to her on the club fender*]
That's a lovely dress.

FLORENCE

It is sweet, isn't it?

TOM

You always wear wonderful clothes.

FLORENCE

Do I, Tom?

TOM

You know you do.

FLORENCE

Do you remember the very first time we met?

TOM

Rather.

FLORENCE

Oxford's so full of romance, isn't it?

TOM

It was when you came down.

FLORENCE

Thank you, Tom dear.

TOM

We did have fun.

FLORENCE

You used to come up to *matinées*, and I'd motor you back afterwards.

TOM

Ripping!

FLORENCE

That reminds me, I've got seats for "Rolling Stones" on Tuesday. Don't forget.

TOM

You never said you were going to get them.

FLORENCE

It doesn't matter. I thought I did. We'd better dine at Claridges.

TOM

But, Florence, I—I can't come!

FLORENCE

Why not?

TOM

I promised to go out.

FLORENCE

Who with?

TOM

Mother.

FLORENCE

Can't you put her off? It will be such a good first night.

TOM

Well—you see, as a matter of fact—it's rather awkward. I put her off the other day——
[*There is a slight pause.*]

FLORENCE

[*A trifle coldly*]
Oh, well, never mind, we'll go some other night.
[*Enter* DAVID.]

DAVID

Hallo, Florence! I thought you were in the drawing-room.

FLORENCE

They're playing Mah-Jong, and there's only one set. I shall break in presently.

TOM

I'll just go and see how they're getting on.
[*This obvious excuse for getting out of the room is not lost upon* FLORENCE.]

FLORENCE

Yes, do.

Tom

Come and play soon.
[*He goes out quietly.*]

Florence

Don't you think this is a divine frock?

David

Very pretty.

Florence

You and Helen seemed to be very thick at dinner.
What were you talking about?

David

Nothing much.   I like Helen.

Florence

Only because she flatters you and listens to everything you say.

David

She doesn't flatter me.

Florence

I suppose she was talking about the farm, and
giving her opinions.

David

We did discuss the farm a little.

FLORENCE

She doesn't know a thing about it, really.

DAVID

Perhaps not, but it passed the time.
[*He goes out.*]
[FLORENCE *sits still for a moment, then she wearily buries her face in her hands. Enter* NICKY.]

NICKY

[*Going to her*]
What's the matter, darling?

FLORENCE

Nothing. I've got a slight headache.

NICKY

Why don't you go Byes?

FLORENCE

I can't; it's much too early.

NICKY

I'm sick of Mah-Jong.

FLORENCE

Who's playing now?

NICKY

Pawnie and Helen and Clara are trying to teach Bruce Fairlight; he's an awful fool at it.
[*He sits down at the piano and plays absently.*]

FLORENCE

You must get Bunty out of that habit of contradicting everything people say.

NICKY

I don't see why.

FLORENCE

It's bad breeding.

NICKY

[*Striking a note viciously*]
Who cares nowadays? We've all got a right to our opinions.

FLORENCE

She seems to forget that I'm much older than she is.

NICKY

That's no argument, mother; it's silly only to remember your age when some one says something you don't like.

FLORENCE

She's having a bad effect on you.

NICKY

Nonsense!

FLORENCE

You've changed since Paris.

NICKY

Naturally.

FLORENCE

You never used to be rude to me.

NICKY

Oh, damn, I'm not rude.

FLORENCE

Yes, you are.

NICKY

Well, don't start running down Bunty.

FLORENCE

Stop playing—stop playing!

NICKY

[*Getting up angrily*]
Oh, God!
[*He goes towards door and collides with* HELEN.]

HELEN

What's happening?

FLORENCE

Nothing. Bunty's just putting Nicky against me.
I knew she'd try to.
[*She goes out.*]

HELEN

You must be having a delightful evening! You
leave the drawing-room, having rowed with Bunty,
and come here and row with Florence.

NICKY

Mother's impossible.

HELEN

She's no different from what she's always been.

NICKY

Well, I haven't realized it before.

HELEN

[*Taking a cigarette and lighting it*]
You haven't been engaged before.

NICKY

I'm hating this house party.

HELEN

[*Lightly*]
Don't say that, dear; it's not kind.

NICKY

You know I don't mean you.

HELEN

Are you very much in love?

NICKY

Yes.—No.—I don't know.

HELEN

I wonder.

NICKY

It's utterly devastating, anyhow.

HELEN

When did you meet her?

NICKY

About five months ago.

HELEN

What was she doing in Paris?

NICKY

Oh, I don't know—fooling about.

HELEN

Splendid.

NICKY

She's been studying French literature.

HELEN

Why?

NICKY

She's going to write—herself—some day.

HELEN

Oh, I see!

NICKY

Helen, do you like her?

HELEN

I can't tell yet—yesterday was the first time I'c
ever set eyes on her.

NICKY

She's wonderfully intelligent.

HELEN

Yes—I'm sure she is.

NICKY

You *don't* like her?

HELEN

I tell you—I'm not sure yet.

NICKY

It's generally the way—one's friends always hate one another.

HELEN

[*Smiling*]
It *is* difficult for you, isn't it?

NICKY

I should so like you to like her.

HELEN

Very well—I'll try.

NICKY

She's utterly opposite to me in every way.

HELEN

Yes, I see that.

NICKY

But that's as it ought to be, isn't it?

HELEN

It depends.

NICKY

I need a sort of restraining influence terribly.

HELEN

Yes, Nicky.

NICKY

She's awfully good for me.

HELEN

Is she?

NICKY

Yes—she curbs me when I get temperamental and silly.

HELEN

I always felt you needed encouraging more than curbing.

NICKY

[*Laughing*]
Oh, Helen—aren't you a darling!

HELEN

I mean it.

NICKY

You're wrong, though—I'm all over the place.

HELEN

Anyhow, I do hope you'll be very happy with her.

NICKY

I don't suppose I shall ever be that.   I haven't got the knack.

HELEN

Do you work hard?

NICKY

Yes.

HELEN

Really hard?

NICKY

Frightfully.

HELEN

Liar!

NICKY

If you'd seen me in Paris—studying, studying—all night long until the gray dawn put the guttering candle to shame—and my nerveless hands dropped from the keys——

HELEN

Candles gutter awfully quickly when they're burned at both ends.

NICKY

Meaning that I look a debauched wreck of my former self?

HELEN

Exactly.

NICKY

If you go on encouraging me at this rate I shall commit suicide.

HELEN

You do resent anyone taking a real interest in you, don't you?

NICKY

I distrust it.

HELEN

Why?

NICKY

I don't know—I'm not worth it.

HELEN

You seem to be suffering from a slight inferiority complex.

NICKY

Not a bit of it—I'm gay and witty and handsome.

HELEN

Oh, Nicky, you're so maddening.

NICKY

Don't be cross, Helen.

HELEN

I'm one of the few people who know what you're really like, and you won't give me the credit for it.

NICKY

Do you think you do, honestly?

HELEN

Yes—and I'm exceedingly worried about you.

NICKY

You needn't be.

HELEN

You're sensitive and reserved and utterly foolish.

NICKY

Thank you—I'm beginning to feel beautifully picturesque.

HELEN

And you're scared.

NICKY

Why! What have I to be scared about?

HELEN

Would you like me to tell you?

NICKY

No.

HELEN

Why not?

NICKY

Because you're a sentimentalist, and you see things that aren't there at all.

HELEN

You're far more sentimental than I.

NICKY

Darling Helen—you've got such a lovely mind—like a Christmas card—with frosted robins and sheep wandering about in the snow—bleating.

HELEN

All the same, I should give up drugs if I were you.

NICKY

Helen!

HELEN

Well?

NICKY

I don't know what you mean.

HELEN

Do you think I can't see?

NICKY

[*Forcing a laugh*]
You're being terribly funny, aren't you?

HELEN

You fool!   You unutterable little fool!

NICKY

Don't be dramatic, dear.

HELEN

I thought you had common sense; I credited you
with more intelligence than that.

NICKY

If you persist in being absurd.

HELEN

[*Suddenly with intense feeling*]

Nicky, don't resist me, don't fight me; I'm your friend; I wouldn't have said a word if I weren't. You've got to stop it; you haven't gone very far yet; there's still time. For God's sake listen to reason.

NICKY

Shut up, shut up, don't speak so loudly.

HELEN

Nicky, throw it away.

NICKY

When did you find out?

HELEN

To-night, you know, when you were playing, but I've guessed for ages.

NICKY

You needn't be frightened, Helen; I only take just the tiniest little bit, once in a blue moon!

HELEN

If anything goes wrong, you'll take a lot. Throw it away.

NICKY

What could go wrong?

HELEN

Never mind, throw it away!

NICKY

I can't. Look out; somebody's coming.
[*Enter* DAVID.]

DAVID

Hallo!

NICKY

Hallo, father!

DAVID

What's the matter?

NICKY

The matter—why?

DAVID

You look very worried.

NICKY

Helen and I have just had a grand heart-to-heart talk; we've undone our back hair, loosened our stays and wallowed in it.

DAVID

Oh, I see!

HELEN

We haven't seen one another for so long—it was inevitable.

DAVID

You never came and looked at the farm this morning. I waited for you.

NICKY

I'm awfully sorry, father—I just went on sleeping.

HELEN

I'll see you later, Nicky.

NICKY

All right.
[HELEN *goes out.*]

DAVID

How do you think your mother's looking?

NICKY

Splendid—the same as ever.

DAVID

Would you like a cigar?

NICKY

No, thanks, father—I'm not very good at them.

DAVID

I was just on my way to bed—there are far too many people in the house.

NICKY

[*Smiling*]
You must be used to that by now.

DAVID

You ought to stay down here, you know—during the week, and get some fresh air.

NICKY

I've got such millions of things to do in London.

DAVID

Worth doing?

NICKY

Yes, of course.

DAVID

You look as though you needed a rest.

NICKY

You needn't worry about me—I feel splendid.

DAVID

She seems a nice girl.

NICKY

Who—Bunty?

DAVID

Yes.   Quiet and untiresome.

NICKY

She's a darling!

DAVID

When do you propose to get married?

NICKY

I don't know.   The engagement's only a sort of try out, you know.

DAVID

Oh, I see.   I didn't realize that.   I'm so unversed in modern technicalities.

NICKY

It's her idea really—just to tread water for a bit.

DAVID

It sounds an excellent plan.

NICKY

I'm awfully glad you like her.

DAVID

Is she musical?

NICKY

Oh, yes—frightfully!

DAVID

Good!

NICKY

Father, I think I will come down here for a few days—and work quietly.

DAVID

If you do that I'll go up to London every other day. I see so little of you when you're at the flat.

NICKY

That's settled then. I wonder what mother will say!

DAVID

I'll talk to her.

NICKY

All right.   She won't bother about us much.

DAVID

No—I don't suppose she will.   I think I'll be
getting along to bed now.   Good night, my boy!

NICKY

Good night, father!
[*They shake hands, and* DAVID *pats* NICKY'S *shoul-
der rather tentatively.   He goes upstairs and*
NICKY *wanders to the piano.   He plays absently,
and* BUNTY *enters.*]

BUNTY

I want to talk to you.

NICKY

[*Still playing*]
All right.

BUNTY

Perhaps you'd stop playing for a minute.

NICKY

Won't you let me woo you with a little Scriabine?

BUNTY

Please stop.

NICKY

[*Rising*]
I'm unappreciated—that's what it is.
[*There is a slight pause—he goes over to her.*]
I say, Bunty——

BUNTY

What?

NICKY

Before you say anything awful to me, I *am* sorry
for being rude just now.

BUNTY

So you ought to be.

NICKY

Will you forgive me?

BUNTY

Yes, I forgive you.

NICKY

I've been irritable all the evening.

BUNTY

Give me a cigarette, Nicky.

NICKY

Here.
[*They both smoke.*]

BUNTY

Thanks.

NICKY

What did you want to talk to me about?

BUNTY

Lots of things——us!

NICKY

[*Hardening*]
Oh, I see!

BUNTY

Don't you think it's rather silly——being engaged?

NICKY

No, not at all.

BUNTY

I do.

NICKY

Just because we bickered a bit to-night?

BUNTY

No, not only because of that.

NICKY

Why then?

BUNTY

Can't you see?

NICKY

No.

BUNTY

Well, we're not very suited to each other, are we?

NICKY

Why do you suddenly say that?

BUNTY

Because I've only just realized it.

NICKY

I'm sorry.

BUNTY

It's not your fault particularly.

NICKY

I'm glad.

BUNTY

It's circumstances and surroundings.

NICKY

Oh, that can be altered quite easily. We'll change the shape of the house—we'll take all that wall away and turn that into a studio—you love studios, don't you?—then we'll transform the drawing-room into an enormous aviary.

BUNTY

It's practically that now!

NICKY

And then we'll——

BUNTY

Shut up, Nicky!

NICKY

I'm only trying to be amenable.

BUNTY

Are you, really?

NICKY

Yes, I'm putting up a sort of defense, Bunty. I have a feeling that you're going to be unpleasant, and I want to establish myself comfortably before you start.

BUNTY

I don't want to be unpleasant—only honest.

NICKY

You won't let the two run together, will you?

BUNTY

[*With vehemence*]
You're hopeless, hopeless, hopeless!

NICKY

Yes—I think I am, rather.

BUNTY

In a way I'm glad—it makes it easier.

NICKY

Does it?

BUNTY

You're not in love with me, really—you couldn't be!

NICKY

Please don't say that.

BUNTY

Why don't you face things properly?

NICKY

One generally has to in the end. I like to put it off for as long as possible.

BUNTY

That's cowardly.

NICKY

Don't be pompous, darling.

BUNTY

You're a great help, I must say.

NICKY

Why should I help to destroy my own happiness?

BUNTY

That's self-pity and self-deception.

NICKY

Why are you going on like this?

BUNTY

Because I tell you—I've realized the truth.

NICKY

I suppose you've taken a hatred to mother!

BUNTY

No, not a hatred.

NICKY

You don't like her.

BUNTY

Not very much.

NICKY

Why not?   She likes you.

BUNTY

She detests me.

NICKY

Nonsense!   Why should she?

BUNTY

Because I'm young.

NICKY

What a filthy thing to say!

BUNTY

It's true.

NICKY

It's nothing of the sort.

BUNTY

You're so stupid sometimes.

NICKY

Thank you.

BUNTY

Don't let's start bickering again.

NICKY

We won't discuss mother any more then

BUNTY

You started it.

NICKY

I wish I could make you understand her like I do. I mean she's awfully irritating, I know—but deep down she's marvelous in spite of everything.

BUNTY

[*Coldly*]
Everything?

NICKY

[*Vehemently*]
Yes, *everything!* Don't be a beast, Bunty; just try to see her point a little, even if you do dislike her. She is terribly silly about being "young," I know, but she's been used to so much admiration and flattery and everything always, she feels she sort of can't give it up—you do see that, don't you? And she hasn't really anything in the least comforting

to fall back upon. She's not clever—real kind of brain cleverness—and father's no good, and I'm no good, and all the time she's wanting life to be as it was instead of as it is. There's no harm in her anywhere—she's just young inside. Can't you imagine the utter foulness of growing old? 'Specially if you've been lovely and attractive like she was. The beautiful Flo Lancaster! She used to be known as that. I can remember her when I was quite small, coming up to say good night to me, looking too perfectly radiant for words—and she used to come to the school, too, sometimes, and everyone used to go mad over her, and I used to get frightfully proud and excited——

BUNTY

I've never heard you talk like this before.

NICKY

I don't think I ever have.

BUNTY

I like you better clear cut, not blurred by sentiment.

[NICKY *looks at her for a moment in amazement.*]

NICKY

To describe you as hard would be inadequate—you're metallic!

BUNTY

I can see straight.

NICKY

[*Politely*]
Can you?

BUNTY

Yes.   We could never be happy together.

NICKY

Perhaps not.

BUNTY

Shall we just—finish—then?

NICKY

Certainly, I'm sorry we were too modern to have
an engagement ring; you'd have been able to give it
back to me so beautifully.

BUNTY

Don't be ridiculous!

NICKY

Better than being blurred by sentiment.
[BUNTY *lights another cigarette and, kicking off her
   shoes, perches on the club fender and proceeds
   to warm her feet at the fire.*]
[*Enter* CLARA HIBBERT.]

CLARA

My dear, I'm *shattered*—and I'm going straight to bed—probably for several weeks.

BUNTY

Why?

CLARA

Shshsh! He's coming.

BUNTY

Who's coming?

CLARA

Bruce Fairlight. I've been teaching him Mah-Jong. These master brains—agony, dear——
[*Enter* BRUCE FAIRLIGHT.]

BRUCE

Very interesting, that game.

CLARA

[*Weakly*]
I thought you'd like it.

BRUCE

It's interesting *psychologically!* The concentration and suspense——

[*Enter* FLORENCE, HELEN, PAWNIE *and* TOM. TOM
   is grasping a whisky and soda—PAWNIE *is eat-
   ing a biscuit.*]

PAWNIE

I'm quite exhausted; it must be the country
air——

FLORENCE

—it was too lovely, because I started with two
red dragons in my hand——

HELEN

I wondered who had them——

PAWNIE

One more tune, Nicky, before we go to bed——

FLORENCE

Yes, just one——

NICKY

[*Looking at* BUNTY]
I'll play "I love you"—such a romantic tune.
[*He puts on the gramophone.*]

BUNTY

Do.

HELEN

What time's everyone going up in the morning?

FLORENCE

The ten-o'clock's the best—we'll have breakfast
t nine downstairs.

PAWNIE

[*Confidentially*]
Do you know that in London I can never do more
han nibble a piece of thin toast, and whenever I'm
way I eat *enormously!*

NICKY

How very peculiar!

PAWNIE

Your tone revolts me, Nicky. You must never be
ascible with your old friends.

NICKY

I haven't got any.

HELEN

Nicky!

NICKY

Sorry, Helen.

FLORENCE

I don't know what's the matter with Nicky. He'
been in a vile temper all the evening—his first week
end home, too.

NICKY

Such a pity, when so much trouble has been taker
to make me happy and cozy.

TOM

Come and dance, Bunty.

BUNTY

No, not now.

NICKY

Dance with him, Bunty. Chaps must have exer
cise.

FLORENCE

You dance with Bunty, Pawnie—I'll dance wit
Tom—come on.
[*She and* TOM *dance.*]

HELEN

The great thing in this world is not to be obviou
Nicky—over *anything!*
[FLORENCE *and* TOM *dance, also* HELEN *and* PAW
NIE. *Everyone talks at once, as in the begin
ning of the act.*]

PAWNIE

You are infuriating, Helen. It's a wonderful book.

HELEN

Thoroughly second-rate.

PAWNIE

What do you think about *Mischievous Passion,* Fairlight?

BRUCE

I never read novels on principle.

PAWNIE

Well, you must read this—it's colossal.

HELEN

Don't be led away by Pawnie, Mr. Fairlight, he has no discrimination.

PAWNIE

But I tell you it's brilliant! Absolutely *brilliant!*

HELEN

Nonsense.

PAWNIE

There are times, Helen, when I could willingly see you dead at my feet.

FLORENCE

A little slower, for Heaven's sake!

NICKY

How's that?
[*He makes it far too slow.*]

FLORENCE

I think you'd better go to bed, Nicky.

HELEN

We're all going, anyhow.

NICKY

Not yet, please, mummy dear——I'm having such a
lovely time!
[*He slams off in a rage.*]

PAWNIE

I always knew the Continent was fatal for the
young.

BUNTY

Nicky's upset——it's my fault——we're not engaged
any more.

FLORENCE

Why——what's happened?

BUNTY

Nothing happened—it was never very serious, really.

HELEN

I had a feeling that it was.

BUNTY

You were wrong.

FLORENCE

Well, I must say it's all been rather abrupt.

BUNTY

It's better to finish things off at once—cleanly—if you're not quite sure, don't you think?

FLORENCE

Well, I'm sorry, Bunty. If you feel like that about it there's nothing more to be said.

BUNTY

I wouldn't have mentioned it at all—only you all seemed to be blaming him for being irritable——

HELEN

Poor Nicky!

CLARA

I really must go up to bed now. I'm so tired. Good night, Florence dear.

FLORENCE

Good night, Clara. Breakfast at nine. Have you got books and everything you want?

CLARA

Yes, thanks. Good night, everyone.
[*Everyone murmurs good night politely.*]

FLORENCE

Tom, be an angel and fetch me a glass of milk It's in the drawing-room.

TOM

All right.
[*He goes off.*]

HELEN

Come on up, Florence. I'm dead.

FLORENCE

So am I. Will you turn out the lights when yo come?

PAWNIE

With beautiful precision, dear.

FLORENCE

[*As she and* HELEN *go upstairs*]
Tell Tom to bring my milk up to me, somebody.

PAWNIE

All right.

FLORENCE

Good night, Mr. Fairlight.

BRUCE

Good night.

PAWNIE

Good night, Florence.
[FLORENCE *and* HELEN *go off.*]

BRUCE

I suppose we'd all better go up.

BUNTY

I don't feel I could sleep yet.
[*Re-enter* TOM *with glass of milk.*]

TOM

Hallo! Where's Florence?

BUNTY

Gone up to bed. Will you take her milk to her?

PAWNIE

What's become of Nicky?

TOM

In the smoking-room, I think.

BRUCE

Good night, Miss Mainwaring.

BUNTY

Good night.
[*They shake hands.*]

PAWNIE

I shall come, too—good night.

TOM

Good night.

PAWNIE

[*To* BRUCE *as they go upstairs*]
When you're writing, do your characters grow as
you go along?

BRUCE

No, I think each one out minutely beforehand.

PAWNIE

How too intriguing.
[*They go off.*]

TOM

So you've broken it off already?

BUNTY

Yes.

TOM

I didn't know you were going to do it so soon.

BUNTY

It's better to get things over.

TOM

What did he say?

BUNTY

Nothing much.

TOM

Was he furious?

BUNTY

Oh, what does it matter?   Don't let's go on about
it.

TOM

It's all damned awkward.

BUNTY

What?

TOM

The whole thing.

BUNTY

You're rather scared, aren't you?

TOM

No, not exactly—now that I've got you to back me up.

BUNTY

I shall be glad when we're out of this house.

TOM

So shall I.

BUNTY

I hate the atmosphere.

TOM

I don't know how I've stood it for so long.

BUNTY

You didn't notice it until I came, any more than I noticed Nicky's atmosphere until you came.

TOM

It's queer, isn't it?

BUNTY

We're reverting to type, don't you see?

TOM

How d'ye mean?

BUNTY

Never mind, it's true.

TOM

Do you think I'm being a cad to Florence?

BUNTY

Yes, I do rather.

TOM

But, Bunty! You said this morning——

BUNTY

That I didn't see how you could help yourself; neither I do. It's frightfully difficult, but it's not altogether your fault, any more than it would have been mine if I'd married Nicky. One gets carried away by glamour, and personality, and magnetism— they're beastly treacherous things.

TOM

You are wonderful.

BUNTY

Don't be silly.

TOM

You're so cool and clear, and you see everything.

BUNTY

I'm sorry—for Nicky.

TOM

Oh, damn Nicky!

BUNTY

[*Laughing*]
Oh, Tom!

TOM

Why, what's up?

BUNTY

You're so dead set.

TOM

You're worth ten of him any day. What's the use of a chap like that? He *doesn't do* anything except play the piano—he can't play any games, he's always trying to be funny——

BUNTY

Shut up, Tom; you're being rather cheap. I haven't reverted to type so quickly that I can't see some of the things I'm missing.

TOM

I wish I knew what you were talking about.

BUNTY

Oh, God! I feel so miserable!
[*She burst into tears.*]

TOM

[*Flummoxed*]
I say—Bunty—for Heaven's sake——
[*He puts his arm round her.*]

BUNTY

[*Shaking him off*]
Don't, don't. Give me my shoes——
[*He picks up her shoes; she puts them on. She is
    half sobbing all the time.*]

TOM

I say, old girl, hadn't you better go to bed?
You're all wrought up!

BUNTY

He said beastly things.

TOM

I'll wring his neck.

BUNTY

[*With a fresh burst of tears*]
Shut up, Tom, shut up——

TOM

Bunty, stop crying—there's a dear; please, please
stop crying——
[*He takes her in his arms and kisses her; she is
groping for her handkerchief.* FLORENCE
comes quietly downstairs.]

BUNTY

I can't find my hanky!

TOM

Here's mine.

FLORENCE

[*Like a pistol shot*]
Tom!
[TOM *and* BUNTY *break away.*]

TOM

Yes, Florence?

FLORENCE

[*Ominously*]
What does this mean?

TOM

I'm sorry, Florence—I——

FLORENCE

You utter cad!

BUNTY

Look here—I should like to say——

FLORENCE

Be quiet—mind your own business.
[NICKY *enters.*]

NICKY

[*Seeing tears on* BUNTY's *face*]
What's the matter—is anybody hurt?

FLORENCE

[*Ominously*]
No, not hurt!

BUNTY

I banged my hand, that's all.

FLORENCE

Liar!

NICKY

Mother—don't be so stupid——

TOM

Florence—I——

FLORENCE

Don't *speak* to me——

NICKY

[*Quietly*]
Mother—not now—not now—it's all wrong. Control yourself! Bunty—Bunty—do go to bed—please.
[*He goes to the piano and begins to play jazz.*]

BUNTY

All right—Tom——
[FLORENCE *goes to the fireplace, trembling with rage.* NICKY *goes on playing.* TOM *and* BUNTY *go towards the stairs.*]

FLORENCE

Stop—I want an explanation, please!

BUNTY

How dare you speak to me like that?

FLORENCE

Get out of my house! Get out of my house!

BUNTY

This is disgusting!

TOM

I say, Florence——

FLORENCE

Get out of my house!

BUNTY

I shall leave the first thing in the morning; it's
much too late tonight.
[*She goes off.*]
[NICKY *never stops playing for a moment.*]

FLORENCE

Tom.   [*He goes towards her, absolutely silent.*]
You kissed her—you kissed her—I saw you!——

TOM

Yes.

FLORENCE

In this house!

TOM

Yes, Florence.   I apologize.

FLORENCE

Apologize! You're beneath contempt. Never speak to me again, never touch me again—I hate you!

TOM

Look here, Florence—I'm desperately sorry. You see, I'm afraid I love her.

FLORENCE

[*Hysterically*]
You dare to stand there and say that to me? It's incredible—after all I've done for you—after all we've been to each other. Love! You don't know what it means. You've lied to me—all these months. It's contemptible—humiliating. Get out of my sight!

TOM

[*Turning and going upstairs*]
Very well.

FLORENCE

[*Suddenly realizing that he is gone*]
Tom—Tom—come back—come back!——
[*She runs upstairs after him. NICKY at last stops playing and lets his hands drop from the keys.*]

CURTAIN

ACT III

ACT III

The scene is FLORENCE'S *bedroom the same night. About two hours have elapsed. When the curtain rises* FLORENCE *is lying face downwards on the bed; she is dressed in a very beautiful but slightly exotic négligé.*

HELEN *is standing by the window, fully dressed; she is holding the curtain aside, and a bar of moonlight comes in to mingle with the amber of the dressing-table lights.* FLORENCE *is obviously extremely hysterical.*

HELEN

Florence, what *is* the use of going on like that?

FLORENCE

I wish I were dead!

HELEN

It's so cowardly to give way utterly—as you're doing.

FLORENCE

I don't care—I don't care!

Helen

If you don't face things in this world, they only hit you much harder in the end.

Florence

He loved me—he adored me!

Helen

Never! He hadn't got it in him.

Florence

After all I've done for him, to go to—to Bunty!

Helen

[*Leaving the window*]
If it hadn't been Bunty it would have been some one else—don't you see how inevitable it was?

Florence

How dared they!—Here!—In this house!

Helen

That's a little thing; it doesn't matter at all.

Florence

It does—it does——

Helen

Florence, sit up and pull yourself together.

FLORENCE

[*Sitting up slowly*]
I think I'm going mad.

HELEN

Not a bit of it; you're just thoroughly hysterical.

FLORENCE

Give me some water.
[HELEN *goes to the bathroom and returns with a glass of water.*]

FLORENCE

[*Taking it*]
What time is it?

HELEN

[*Looking at her watch*]
Ten past one.

FLORENCE

Don't go to London by the early train, Helen; stay and come up with me in the car.

HELEN

Very well.

FLORENCE

Thank God, you were here!

HELEN

I wish I'd known what was happening; I might have done something.

FLORENCE

What can I do to get him back?

HELEN

Don't be silly.

FLORENCE

What can I do—what can I do?——

HELEN

Do you mean to say you'd *take* him back after to-night?

FLORENCE

No, never.   Not if he crawled to me—never——

HELEN

Well, then, make up your mind definitely never to see him again whatever happens.

FLORENCE

Yes—I will.

HELEN

Why don't you go to bed now?

FLORENCE

I couldn't sleep.

HELEN

Put it all out of your mind—make an effort.

FLORENCE

I can't—I'm too unhappy.

HELEN

Think of Nicky.

FLORENCE

Nicky's young.

HELEN

That doesn't make it any better for him.

FLORENCE

He'll get over it in the long run.

HELEN

The long run never counts at the moment.

FLORENCE

He wasn't in love—really?

HELEN

As much as either you or he are capable of it.

FLORENCE

He's well rid of her. She'd never have appreciated him properly—she hasn't the intelligence.

HELEN

I don't agree with you there—she's got intelligence right enough.

FLORENCE

Treacherous little beast!

HELEN

Yes, but far-seeing.

FLORENCE

Are you standing up for her? Do you think it was *right* of her to get Tom away from me?

HELEN

Yes, quite right.

FLORENCE

Helen!

HELEN

To do her justice, she didn't deliberately set herself out to get him away from you at all. She discovered that in spite of the somewhat decadent years Tom was still her type, and likely to remain so. So with common sense she decided to shelve Nicky forthwith and go for him.

FLORENCE

Her type indeed!

HELEN

Yes, she'd have been quite a nice girl really if she'd been left alone and not allowed to go to Paris and get into the wrong set.

FLORENCE

You are extraordinary, Helen. Do you realize that you're making excuses for the girl who's betrayed your best friend?

HELEN

Don't be so utterly absurd. I'm not making excuses, and, anyhow, she hasn't betrayed you. She hardly knows you, in the first place, and she's just followed her instincts regardless of anyone else's feelings—as you've done thousands of times.

FLORENCE

Helen—you're being horrible to me!

HELEN

I'm not, I'm trying to make you see! You're battering your head against silly cast-iron delusions, and I want to dislodge them.

FLORENCE

Helen, I'm so unhappy—so desperately unhappy.

HELEN

Yes, but not because you've lost Tom; it's something far deeper than that.

FLORENCE

What then?

HELEN

You're on the wrong tack, and have been for years.

FLORENCE

I don't understand.

HELEN

You *won't* understand!

[FLORENCE *gets off the bed and goes over to the dressing-table. She sits and stares at herself in the glass for a moment without speaking.*]

FLORENCE

My eyes are sore. [*She powders her face and sprays a little scent on her hair.*] It's so lovely this—and so refreshing.

HELEN

I think I'll go to bed now.

FLORENCE

No, wait a little longer with me—please, Helen—just a few minutes.

HELEN

It's so hot in here.

FLORENCE

Open the window then.

HELEN

All right.
[*She goes to the window and opens it.* FLORENCE
*takes a cigarette out of a box and then shakes
a scent-bottle and rubs the cigarette lightly
with the stopper.*]

FLORENCE

Do you ever do this? It's divine.

HELEN

What a wonderfully clear night. You can see the hills right across the valley—the moon's quite strong.
[FLORENCE *goes to the window and stands next to*
HELEN, *looking out—she is puffing her ciga-
rette.*]

FLORENCE

I chose this room in the first place because the view was so lovely.

HELEN

Do you ever look at it?

FLORENCE

[*Listlessly*]
Of course I do, often!

HELEN

It's been raining.   I wish you'd throw away that cigarette—it spoils the freshness.

FLORENCE

[*Turning away*]
It's soothing me—calming my nerves.

HELEN

I do wish I could help you—really!

FLORENCE

You are helping me, darling—you're being an angel.

HELEN

[*Suddenly angry*]
Don't talk so emptily, Florence; I'm worth more than that.

FLORENCE

I don't know what you mean.

HELEN

It sickens me to see you getting back so soon.

FLORENCE

Getting back?

HELEN

Yes, to your usual worthless attitude of mind.

FLORENCE

Helen!

HELEN

A little while ago you were really suffering for once, and in a way I was glad because it showed you were capable of a genuine emotion. Now you're glossing it over—swarming it down with your returning vanity; soon you won't be unhappy any more—just vindictive.

FLORENCE

Don't go on at me like that—I'm too wretched.

HELEN

[*Going to her*]
Florence dear, forgive me, but it's true—and I don't want it to be.

[*The door opens and* NICKY *enters.   He is in dressing-gown and pyjamas.   His face looks strained and white.*]

FLORENCE

Nicky!

NICKY

Helen, I want to talk to mother, please.

HELEN

All right, Nicky.

FLORENCE

What is it?

NICKY

I couldn't sleep.

HELEN

Florence dear—good night.

FLORENCE

No—no, Helen—don't go yet——

HELEN

I must.

FLORENCE

Helen—stay with me.

NICKY

Please go.

HELEN

I can't stay, Florence—it's quite impossible.
[*She goes out.*]

FLORENCE

I don't know what you mean—by coming here and ordering Helen out of my room.

NICKY

I'm sorry, mother. I felt I had to talk to you alone.

FLORENCE

At this hour of the night? You're mad!

NICKY

No, I'm not; I think I'm probably more unhappy than I've ever been in my life.

FLORENCE

You're young—you'll get over it.

NICKY

I hope so.

FLORENCE

I knew the first moment I saw her—what sort of a girl she was.

NICKY

Oh, mother!

FLORENCE

It's true.   I had an *instinct* about her.

NICKY

It's all been rather a shock, you know——

FLORENCE

[*Becoming motherly*]
Yes, dear—I know—I know—but you mustn'
be miserable about her; she isn't worth it.   [*She
goes to kiss him.*]

NICKY

[*Gently pushing her away*]
Don't, mother!

FLORENCE

Listen, Nicky.   Go back to bed now—there's ε
dear; my head's splitting.

NICKY

I can't yet.

FLORENCE

Take some aspirin; that'll calm your nerves.

NICKY

I'm afraid I'm a little beyond aspirin.

FLORENCE

I don't want you to think I don't sympathize with you, darling—my heart *aches* for you—I know so well what you're going through.

NICKY

Do you?

FLORENCE

It's agony—absolute agony—but, you see—it will wear off—it always does in time. [NICKY *doesn't answer.*] Nicky, please go now!

NICKY

I want to talk to you.

FLORENCE

To-morrow—we'll talk to-morrow.

NICKY

No, now—*now!*

FLORENCE

You're inconsiderate and cruel—I've told you my head's bursting.

NICKY

I want to sympathize with you, too—and try t
understand everything—as well as I can——

FLORENCE

Understand everything?

NICKY

Yes, please.

FLORENCE

I don't know what you mean——

NICKY

Will you tell me things—as though I were som
body quite different?

FLORENCE

What kind of things?

NICKY

Things about you—your life.

FLORENCE

Really, Nicky—you're ridiculous—asking me
tell you stories at this hour!

Nicky

[*With dead vehemence*]
Mother—sit down quietly. I'm not going out of this room until I've got everything straight in my mind.

Florence

[*Sinking down—almost hypnotized*]
Nicky—please—I——

Nicky

Tom Veryan has been your lover, hasn't he?

Florence

[*Almost shrieking*]
Nicky—how dare you!

Nicky

Keep calm—it's our only chance—keep calm.

Florence

[*Bursting into tears*]
How dare you speak to me like that—suggest such a thing! I——

Nicky

It's true, isn't it?

Florence

Go away—go away!

NICKY

It's true, isn't it?

FLORENCE

No—no!

NICKY

It's true, isn't it?

FLORENCE

No—I tell you—no—no—no!

NICKY

You're lying to me, mother. What's the use of that?

FLORENCE

You're mad—mad——

NICKY

Does father know?

FLORENCE

Go away!

NICKY

Does father know?

FLORENCE

Your father knows nothing—he doesn't understand me any more than you do.

NICKY

Then it's between us alone.

FLORENCE

I tell you I don't know what you're talking about.

NICKY

Mother—don't go on like that; it's useless. We've arrived at a crisis; wherever we go—whatever we do we can't escape from it. I know we're neither of us very strong-minded or capable, and we haven't much hope of coming through successfully—but let's try. It's no good pretending any more—our lives are built up of pretenses all the time. For years—ever since I began to think at all, I've been bolstering up my illusions about you. People have made remarks, not realizing that I was your son, and I've pretended that they were inspired by cattiness and jealousy. I've noticed things—trivial incriminating little incidents, and I've brushed them aside and not thought any more about them because you were my mother—clever and beautiful and successful—and naturally people *would* slander you *because* you

were so beautiful—and now I *know*—they were
right!

FLORENCE

Nicky—I implore you—go away now—leave me
alone.

NICKY

No, I can't.

FLORENCE

You're cruel—cruel to torment me——

NICKY

I don't want to be cruel——

FLORENCE

Go to bed then, and we'll talk everything over
quietly another time.

NICKY

It is true about Tom Veryan, isn't it?

FLORENCE

No. No——

NICKY

We're on awfully dangerous ground. I'm strain-
ing every nerve to keep myself under control. If

you lie to me and try to evade me any more—I won't
be answerable for what might happen.

FLORENCE

[*Dropping her voice—terrified*]
What do you mean?

NICKY

I don't know—I'm frightened.

FLORENCE

Nicky—darling Nicky—I——
[*She approaches him.*]

NICKY

Don't touch me, please.

FLORENCE

Have a little pity for me.

NICKY

Was Tom Veryan your lover?

FLORENCE

[*In a whisper*]
Yes.

NICKY

I want to understand why——

FLORENCE

He loved me.

NICKY

But you—did you love him?

FLORENCE

Yes.

NICKY

It was something you couldn't help, wasn't it—
something that's always been the same in you since
you were quite, quite young?——

FLORENCE

Yes, Nicky—yes——

NICKY

And there have been others, too, haven't there?

FLORENCE

[*With her face in her hands*]
I won't be cross-questioned any more—I won't—
I won't——

NICKY

I wish you'd understand I'm not blaming you—
I'm trying to help you—to help us both——

FLORENCE

What good can all this possibly do?

NICKY

Clear things up, of course. I can't go on any
more half knowing——

FLORENCE

Why should that side of my life be any concern
of yours?

NICKY

But, mother!

FLORENCE

I'm different from other women—completely different—and you expect me to be the same. Why
can't you realize that with a temperament like mine
it's impossible to live an ordinary humdrum life.
You're not a boy any longer—you're a man—
and——

NICKY

I'm nothing—I've grown up all wrong.

FLORENCE

It's not my fault.

NICKY

Of course it's your fault, mother—who else's fault
could it be?

FLORENCE

Your friends—the people you mix with——

NICKY

It wouldn't matter *who* I mixed with if only I had
a background.

FLORENCE

You've got as much money as you want—you've
got your home——

NICKY

[*Bitterly*]
Home! That's almost funny—there's no peace
anywhere—nothing but the ceaseless din of trying
to be amused——

FLORENCE

David never complains.

NICKY

I don't suppose you've looked at father during the
last few years—or you wouldn't say that.

Florence

He's perfectly happy because he's sensible—he
lives his own life and doesn't try to interfere with
mine.

Nicky

It must be your vanity that makes you so dreadfully blind—and foolish.

Florence

Understand once and for all, I *won't* be spoken to
like this——

Nicky

You've had other lovers besides Tom Veryan—
haven't you?

Florence

Yes, I have—I have. Now then!

Nicky

Well, anyhow—that's the truth—at last——
[*He rises, turns his back on her and stands looking
out of the window.*]

Florence

[*After a pause—going to him*]
Nicky—don't be angry—please don't be angry
with me.

NICKY

I'm not angry a bit. I realize that I'm living in a world where things like this happen—and they've got to be faced and given the right value. If only I'd had the courage to realize everything before— it wouldn't be so bad now. It's the sudden shock that's thrown the whole thing out of focus for me— but I mean to get it right. Please help me!

FLORENCE

[*Dully*]
I don't know what to do.

NICKY

It's your life, and you've lived it as you've wanted to live it—that's fair——

FLORENCE

Yes—yes.

NICKY

You've wanted love always—passionate love, because you were made like that. It's not your fault— it's the fault of circumstances and civilization; civilization makes rottenness so much easier. We're utterly rotten—both of us——

FLORENCE

Nicky—don't—don't——

NICKY

How can we help ourselves? We swirl about in a vortex of beastliness. This is a chance—don't you see—to realize the truth—our only chance.

FLORENCE

Oh, Nicky, do stop—go away!

NICKY

Don't keep on telling me to stop when our only hope is to hammer it out.

FLORENCE

You're overwrought. It isn't as bad as you think.

NICKY

Isn't it?

FLORENCE

No, no. Of course it isn't. To-morrow morning you'll see things quite differently.

NICKY

You haven't understood.

FLORENCE

Yes, I have—I have.

NICKY

You haven't understood. Oh, my God, you haven't understood! You're building up silly defenses in your mind. I'm overwrought. To-morrow morning I shall see things quite differently. That's true— that's the tragedy of it, and you won't see. To-morrow morning I *shall* see things quite differently. All this will seem unreal—a nightmare—the machinery of our lives will go on again and gloss over the truth as it always does—and our chance will be gone forever.

FLORENCE

Chance—chance? What are you talking about— what chance?

NICKY

I must make you see, somehow.

FLORENCE

You're driving me mad.

NICKY

Have patience with me—please—please——

FLORENCE

[*Wildly*]
How can I have patience with you? You exaggerate everything.

NICKY

No I don't—I wish I did.

FLORENCE

Listen—let me explain something to you.

NICKY

Very well—go on.

FLORENCE

You're setting yourself up in judgment on me—
your own mother.

NICKY

No, I'm not.

FLORENCE

You are—you are. Let me speak. You don't
understand my temperament in the least—nobody
does—I——

NICKY

You're deceiving yourself—your temperament's
no different from thousands of other women, but
you've been weak and selfish and given way all along
the line——

FLORENCE

Let me speak, I tell you!——

NICKY

What's the use? You're still pretending—you're building up barriers between us instead of helping me to break them down.

FLORENCE

What are you accusing me of having done?

NICKY

Can't you see yet?

FLORENCE

No, I can't. If you're preaching morality, you've no right to. That's my affair—I've never done any harm to anyone.

NICKY

Look at me.

FLORENCE

Why—what do you mean?

NICKY

You've given me *nothing* all my life—nothing that counts.

FLORENCE

Now you're pitying yourself.

Nicky

Yes, with every reason.

Florence

You're neurotic and ridiculous. Just because Bunty broke off your engagement you come and say wicked, cruel things to me——

Nicky

You forget what I've seen to-night, mother.

Florence

I don't care what you've seen.

Nicky

I've seen you make a vulgar, disgusting scene in your own house, and on top of that humiliate yourself before a boy half your age. The misery of losing Bunty faded away when that happened—. everything is comparative, after all.

Florence

I didn't humiliate myself——

Nicky

You ran after him up the stairs because your vanity wouldn't let you lose him. It isn't that you love him—that would be easier—you never love any-

one, you only love them loving you—all your so-
called passion and temperament is false—your whole
existence had degenerated into an endless empty
craving for admiration and flattery—and then you
say you've done no harm to anybody. Father used
to be a clever man, with a strong will and a capacity
for enjoying everything—I can remember him like
that—and now he's nothing—a complete nonentity
because his spirit's crushed. How could it be other-
wise? You've let him down consistently for years—
and God knows I'm nothing for him to look forward
to—but I might have been if it hadn't been for
you——

FLORENCE

Don't talk like that. Don't—don't. It can't be
such a crime being loved—it can't be such a crime
being happy——

NICKY

You're not happy—you're never happy—you're
fighting—fighting all the time to keep your youth
and your looks—because you can't bear the thought
of living without them—as though they mattered
in the end.

FLORENCE

[*Hysterically*]
What does anything matter—ever?

NICKY

That's what I'm trying to find out.

FLORENCE

I'm still young inside—I'm still beautiful. Why houldn't I live my life as I choose?

NICKY

You're not young or beautiful; I'm seeing for the rst time how old you are. It's horrible— our silly fair hair—and your face all plastered and ainted——

FLORENCE

Nicky—Nicky—stop—stop—stop!
She flings herself face downwards on the bed.
    NICKY *goes over to her.*]

NICKY

Mother!

FLORENCE

Go away—go away—I hate you—go away——

NICKY

Mother—sit up——

FLORENCE

[*Pulling herself together*]
Go out of my room——

NICKY

Mother——

FLORENCE

I don't ever want to see you again—you're insane —you've said wicked, wicked things to me—you've talked to me as though I were a woman off the streets. I can't bear any more—I can't bear any more!

NICKY

I have a slight confession to make——

FLORENCE

Confession?

NICKY

Yes.

FLORENCE

Go away—go away——

NICKY

[*Taking a small gold box from his pocket*] Look——

FLORENCE

What do you mean—what is it——?

NICKY

Don't you know?

[FLORENCE *takes the box with trembling fingers and opens it. She stares at it for a moment. When she speaks again her voice is quite dead.*]

FLORENCE

Nicky, it isn't—you haven't——?

NICKY

Why do you look so shocked?

FLORENCE

[*Dully*]
Oh, my God!

NICKY

What does it matter?

[FLORENCE *suddenly rises and hurls the box out of the window.*]

That doesn't make it any better.

FLORENCE

[*Flinging herself on her knees beside him*]
Nicky, promise me, oh, promise you'll never do it again—never in your life—it's frightful—hor-rible——

NICKY

It's only just the beginning.

FLORENCE

What can I say to you—what can I say to you?

NICKY

Nothing—under the circumstances.

FLORENCE

What do you mean?

NICKY

It can't possibly matter—now.

FLORENCE

Matter—but it's the finish of everything—you're young, you're just starting on your life—you must stop—you must swear never to touch it again—swear to me on your oath, Nicky—I'll help you—I'll help you——

NICKY

You!
[*He turns away.*]

FLORENCE

[*Burying her face in her hands and moaning*]
Oh—oh—oh!

NICKY

How could you possibly help me?

FLORENCE

[*Clutching him*]
Nicky!

NICKY

[*Almost losing control*]
Shut up——shut up——don't touch me——

FLORENCE

[*Trying to take him in her arms*]
Nicky——Nicky——

NICKY

I'm trying to control myself, but you won't let me——you're an awfully rotten woman, really.

FLORENCE

Nicky——stop——stop——stop——
[*She beats him with her fists.*]

NICKY

Leave go of me!
[*He breaks away from her, and going up to the dressing-table he sweeps everything off on to the floor with his arm.*]

FLORENCE

[*Screaming*]
Oh——oh——Nicky——!

NICKY

Now then! Now then! You're not to have any
more lovers; you're not going to be beautiful and
successful ever again—you're going to be my mother
for once—it's about time I had one to help me, before
I go over the edge altogether——

FLORENCE

Nicky—Nicky——

NICKY

Promise me to be different—you've got to promise
me!

FLORENCE

[*Sinking on to the end of couch, facing audience*]
Yes—yes—I promise—— [*The tears are running
down her face.*]

NICKY

I love you, really—that's why it's so awful.
[*He falls on his knees by her side and buries his face
in her lap.*]

FLORENCE

No. No, not awful—don't say that—I love you,
too.

NICKY

[*Sobbing hopelessly*]
Oh, mother——!

FLORENCE

[*Staring in front of her*]
I wish I were dead!

NICKY

It doesn't matter about death, but it matters terribly about life.

FLORENCE

I know——

NICKY

[*Desperately*]
Promise me you'li be different—promise me you'll be different——

FLORENCE

Yes, yes—I'll try——

NICKY

We'll both try.

FLORENCE

Yes, dear.—Oh, my dear——!
[*She sits quite still, staring in front of her—the tears are rolling down her cheeks, and she is stroking* NICKY'S *hair mechanically in an effort to calm him.*]

CURTAIN